BEWARE!
KILLER PLANTS

INTOXICATING PLANTS

by Joyce Markovics

 CHERRY LAKE PRESS
Ann Arbor, Michigan

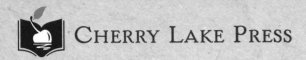
CHERRY LAKE PRESS

Published in the United States of America by Cherry Lake Publishing Group
Ann Arbor, Michigan
www.cherrylakepublishing.com

Reading Adviser: Beth Walker Gambro, MS Ed., Reading Consultant, Yorkville, IL
Content Adviser: Angie Andrade, Senior Horticulturist, Denver Botanic Gardens
Book Designer: Ed Morgan

Photo Credits: © Chaicom/Shutterstock, cover and title page; Public Domain, 4; © Manfred Ruckszio/Shutterstock, 5; © lostkutnikov/Shutterstock, 6–7; Dominique Jacquin, Wikimedia Commons, 7; Public Domain, 8; Public Domain, 9 top; © freepik.com, 9 bottom; © Matt Hahnewald/Shutterstock, 10 top; © Al.geba/Shutterstock, 10 bottom; © Zonjang2499/Shutterstock, 11; LBM1948, Wikimedia Commons, 12; © Lotus Images/Shutterstock, 13 top; © Karan Bunjean/Shutterstock, 13 bottom; © Chrispo/Shutterstock, 14; © COULANGES/Shutterstock, 15 left; Wikimedia Commons, 15 right; Public Domain, 16; Public Domain, 17; © Cindy Creighton/Shutterstock, 18; © Vita Serendipity/Shutterstock, 19; © Vlad Siaber/Shutterstock, 20; © bogdan ionescu/Shutterstock, 21; Lip Kee Yap, Wikimedia Commons, 22.

Cherry Lake Press is an imprint of Cherry Lake Publishing Group.

Library of Congress Cataloging-in-Publication Data

Names: Markovics, Joyce L., author.
Title: Intoxicating plants / by Joyce Markovics.
Description: Ann Arbor, Michigan : Cherry Lake Publishing, [2021] | Series:
  Beware! killer plants | Includes bibliographical references and index. |
  Audience: Grades 4-6
Identifiers: LCCN 2021001267 (print) | LCCN 2021001268 (ebook) | ISBN
  9781534187689 (hardcover) | ISBN 9781534189089 (paperback) | ISBN
  9781534190481 (pdf) | ISBN 9781534191884 (ebook)
Subjects: LCSH: Poisonous plants—Juvenile literature. | Dangerous
  plants—Juvenile literature.
Classification: LCC QK100.A1 M376 2021 (print) | LCC QK100.A1 (ebook) |
  DDC 581.6/59—dc23
LC record available at https://lccn.loc.gov/2021001267
LC ebook record available at https://lccn.loc.gov/2021001268

Printed in the United States of America
Corporate Graphics

CONTENTS

DANCING ILLNESS

More than 1,000 years ago, a strange illness gripped people in the French countryside. They wandered around confused. Their bodies twisted and shook as if they were dancing. Some felt burning pains in their hands and feet. In the worst cases, their fingers, toes, and ears turned black—and fell off.

Artwork showing people sickened by the mystery illness

Due to the burning pains, people called the illness Holy Fire. At the time, no one knew that the people had been sickened by ergot. This toxic fungus grows on plants such as wheat.

The black growths on this wheat plant are ergot, the toxic fungi.

WARNING: Plants can be dangerous. Never touch or eat an unfamiliar plant.

Ergot also grows on rye and other grain plants often used to make bread. The fungus thrives after heavy rains. When ergot first attacks, it causes the plants to ooze yellow goo. This sticky liquid helps spread the fungus. Then ergot sends out many thin, dark threads.

These threads cover the grain, turning it into a purplish-black growth called a sclerotium (skli-ROH-shee-uhm). The sclerotium looks like a dark-colored grain. Farmers easily can mistake it for a healthy grain. However, anyone who eats the grain can become very sick.

Ergot sclerotia mixed with healthy grains

Other ergot outbreaks have happened over the years. Some experts believe one took place in early 1692 in Salem, Massachusetts. At the time, eight girls started acting strangely. They babbled, shook wildly, and their skin felt tingly. The townspeople believed the girls were under a witch's spell!

A print showing one of the sick girls in Salem

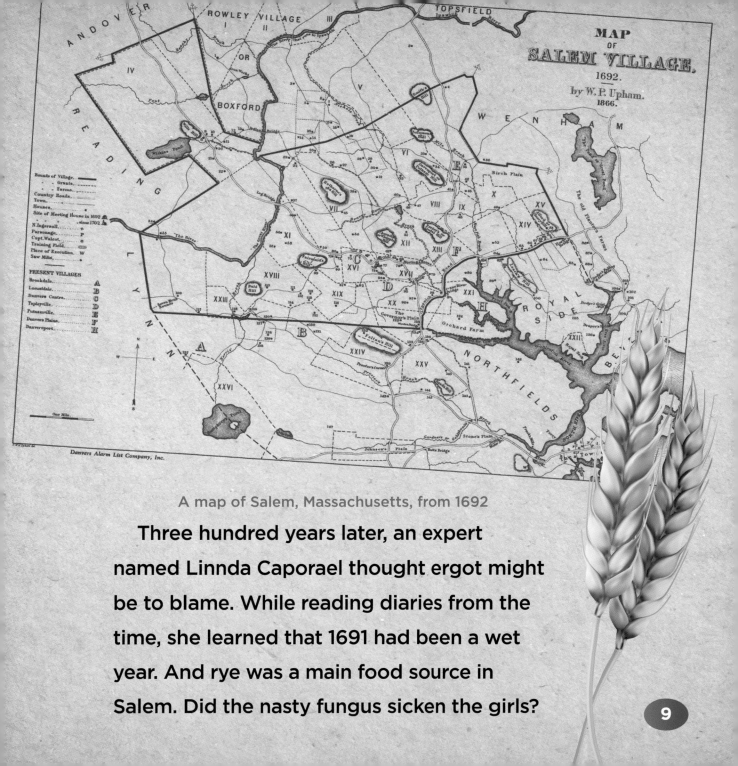

A map of Salem, Massachusetts, from 1692

Three hundred years later, an expert named Linnda Caporael thought ergot might be to blame. While reading diaries from the time, she learned that 1691 had been a wet year. And rye was a main food source in Salem. Did the nasty fungus sicken the girls?

FOUL BETEL NUTS

Intoxicating plants grow all over the world. In India and other parts of Asia, millions of people can be seen chewing and spitting. Their saliva is dark red like a brick. It stains the ground at their feet. What's the reason for this behavior? The surprising answer is the betel nut palm tree.

A betel nut chewer

Red saliva from a betel nut chewer

The betel nut palm is a tall, slim tree that grows in tropical forests. The tree produces small fruits about the size of chicken eggs. The seeds inside the fruits are known as betel nuts.

The betel nut palm is also called the areca palm.

People collect the betel palm's seeds. They slice the fruit and wrap it in a leaf from another plant, the betel vine. In fact, the betel nut palm tree gets its name from the vine. Sometimes, people also tuck spices inside the leaf.

Betel seeds

Betel nut chewers pop the little leafy package inside their mouths. It has a fresh, peppery taste. Chemicals in the plants make the chewer feel alert as well as dizzy. These chemicals also cause people to produce lots of red saliva. Many people become **addicted** to chewing the nuts.

Seeds and betel leaves before they're chewed

Over time, a chewer's teeth can turn black!

Chewing betel nuts can cause serious illnesses like cancer.

SCREAMING MANDRAKE

The mandrake is another intoxicating plant. Above ground, it looks ordinary with its crown of green leaves and bell-shaped flowers. Underground, its root is anything but typical. A mandrake's forked root can grow up to 4 feet (1.2 meters) long. It's curvy and hairy. To some, it looks like a small human body!

Mandrakes grow in Europe and the Middle East.

Because of its humanlike shape, people long ago thought the mandrake was magical. They believed the plant would scream if pulled from the ground. The shrieks were said to be so loud that they could somehow kill a person.

The mandrake is also known as manroot.

Mandragoras.

1.

2.

FOEMINA

MARIS

Witches were said to put mandrake in their potions. The plant is mentioned in the book *Harry Potter and the Chamber of Secrets*. Harry and his friends learn about the mandrake's magical powers. They're warned of the fatal screams of the plant, which looks like a human baby when young.

An illustration of a humanlike mandrake root from an ancient book

The playwright William Shakespeare refers to the mandrake in his play *Romeo and Juliet*. The potion that puts Juliet to sleep may have been made from the root.

Despite many **myths** about the mandrake, people learned it had actual powers. The root contains many chemicals that can affect the brain. The chemicals can relieve pain, cause dizziness, and even lead to a **coma**. "If the dose is high enough, it could kill you," says scientist Michael Heinrich.

The mandrake is one of about 2,500 plants in the nightshade family. These plants include tomatoes, peppers, and eggplant.

Menacing Mushrooms

Mushrooms aren't true plants. They are fungi like ergot. But they hold a top spot in the world of intoxicating **organisms**. Over the years, mushrooms have poisoned tens of thousands of people. Some are extremely toxic.

Inky cap mushrooms are very toxic.

Fly agaric and other mushrooms sometimes grow in a circle.
This is known as a fairy ring—or ring of death.

One of the most recognized mushrooms is the fly agaric. This attractive mushroom is reddish-orange with white spots. It's often shown in books of fairy tales. But it's far from harmless. If eaten, it can cause dizziness, confusion, coma, and death!

In 1996, more than 100 people died in the Ukraine after eating mushrooms they found in a forest.

One killer mushroom is responsible for more deaths than any other—the death cap mushroom. This small, light-colored mushroom often tricks people. Why? It looks like a common paddy straw mushroom that's safe to eat.

Death cap mushrooms

Death cap mushrooms are found throughout North America and Europe. People usually get sick between 6 and 24 hours after eating one. The first sign of poisoning is an upset stomach. Then the mushroom causes fatal liver damage. Only half of a death cap mushroom can kill an adult human!

The false morel mushroom looks like its edible cousin. However, it can cause severe pain and harm the kidneys.

WARNING: Never touch or eat a mushroom you find outside. It might be toxic.

PLANT PARTNERS

Plants and animals sometimes help one another. This type of relationship is called mutualism.

In Malaysia, long-tailed parakeets and betel nut palms have a close relationship. The parakeets feed on the palm's tasty fruit. When they do so, they move seeds away from the parent tree. Over time, this action allows new trees to grow. The birds' poop also acts as a fertilizer for the tree.

Betel Nut Palm

Betel nut palms produce tasty fruit that attracts long-tailed parakeets.

Long-Tailed Parakeet

Long-tailed parakeets eat the fruit of the betel nut palm. As they do, they help the tree to spread its seeds, which grow into new trees.

GLOSSARY

addicted (uh-DIK-tid) unable to stop doing or using something

coma (KOH-muh) a state in which a person is unconscious and cannot wake up; can be caused by toxins

ergot (UR-guht) a fungal disease of rye and other grain plants

fatal (FAY-tuhl) deadly

fertilizer (FUR-tuh-lyze-ur) a chemical or natural substance added to the soil that helps plants grow

fungus (FUHN-guhss) a plantlike organism that can't make its own food, such as a mushroom

intoxicating (in-TOK-suh-kayt-ing) causing someone to lose control of their body and behavior

myths (MITHS) widely held but false beliefs

organisms (OR-guh-niz-uhmz) living things

outbreaks (OUT-brayks) sudden rises in the occurrence of something, such as a disease

saliva (suh-LYE-vuh) a clear liquid produced in the mouths of humans that helps them swallow and chew; also called spit

tingly (TING-lee) causing a slight prickly or stinging feeling

toxic (TOK-sik) poisonous

Find Out More

Books

Hirsch, Rebecca E. *When Plants Attack: Strange and Terrifying Plants*. Minneapolis: Millbrook Press, 2019.

Lawler, Janet. *Scary Plants*. New York: Penguin Young Readers, 2017.

Thorogood, Chris. *Perfectly Peculiar Plants*. Lake Forest, CA: Words & Pictures, 2018.

Websites

The Alnwick Garden: The Poison Garden
   https://www.alnwickgarden.com/the-garden/poison-garden/

Britannica: Betel
   https://www.britannica.com/plant/betel#ref188422

U.S. Forest Service—The Powerful Solanaceae: Mandrake
   https://www.fs.fed.us/wildflowers/ethnobotany/Mind_and_Spirit/mandrake.shtml

Index

About The Author

Joyce Markovics enjoys writing about and collecting unusual plants. One of her favorites is a hardy coffee plant with very glossy leaves that lives on a shelf in her bathroom.